I0453762

Man Enough for Myself

Man Enough for Myself

*A Poetry Collection by
D. Dreakford*

© 2025 D. Dreakford

All rights reserved. No part of this book may be reproduced or transmitted in any form or by any means, electronic or mechanical, including photocopying, recording, or by any information storage and retrieval system, without prior written permission of the publisher, except for brief quotations in reviews or critical articles.

ISBN: 979-8-9935001-1-9 (paperback)
ISBN: 979-8-9935001-3-3 (D2D paperback)
ISBN: 979-8-9935001-0-2 (hardcover)
ISBN: 979-8-9935001-2-6 (eBook)

First Edition, 2025

Independently published by Donatello Dreakford

Cover design by the author
Interior design by the author
Edited by the author

This is a memoir told from the author's perspective. Some names and identifying details have been changed to protect privacy.

This book is for my family.

The one I was born into, and the one I built.

To my father, my biggest supporter, who reminds me I don't have to carry everything alone, and to my brothers T and J.

To my daughter Angel, my little sister Pixie, my queer mother Keelan, and my sister Venus, you are the heart of the family I chose.

To Celeste, Kamakshya, Vana, Xian, and Nate, who each held a part of me when I didn't know if there was anything left worth holding.

And to my partner Tina, for loving me in a way that feels safe, steady, and real. You've shown me what it means to be cared for without having to earn it.

I love you all more than words can say.

Contents:

Preface

When I started writing this book, I didn't know exactly what it would become. I only knew I couldn't keep carrying everything alone. What began as scattered notes and half-finished poems turned into a map of my life. Not just the obvious parts like gender transition or trauma recovery, but the smaller, harder to explain moments. The in-betweens. The silences. The parts of me I used to think weren't worth remembering because they didn't fit into a clear narrative or serve a larger purpose.

This isn't a clean story, and I don't have a thesis to argue or a resolution to offer. I'm not here to explain transness or justify my manhood. I'm certainly not writing from a place of having figured it all out. I'm writing from inside the process. From the mess, the grief, the hunger, the staying. From all the selves I've been, and all the versions I've tried to kill off or carry forward. Some of it slow and quiet, some of it painful and unfinished.

You'll meet the people who helped me keep going, and the ones I had to leave behind. You'll hear the voice of the boy I fought to become, and the echoes of the girl I used to be. You'll see what it means to try, again and again, to stay.

This book is my very first. For years I dreamed of being a writer, but life always made it feel impossible. Poverty, grief, addiction, survival, all of it kept pushing my words to the side. I wrote in notebooks I couldn't hold onto, in phone notes that disappeared, in scraps that never made it past a single line. I wrote without thinking anyone would ever read it, my own secret little way to keep breathing when silence pressed too heavy on my chest. It was private. It was only for me.

I never imagined I would gather those words into something like this. That I would have the chance to sit here and hand them to someone else. That is why holding this book feels like holding a piece of my own staying in my hands, and now in yours. It feels like proof that I am still here, still speaking, and still making something out of everything I thought would end me.

And it feels urgent. Given the state of the world right now, it is not a neutral act for someone like me to speak. The world at large has always wanted people like me, Black people, transgender people, and queer people, to disappear. To be erased, silenced, or made invisible. Putting this story out there is my refusal of that erasure. It is my way of insisting on being seen, of leaving a trace, of saying that our lives and our words matter.

You'll notice the book moves in fragments. Poems, confessions, flashbacks, love letters. It doesn't follow a strict timeline, because neither does living. Instead, it moves like memory does. Circling back, repeating, skipping around until the shape of it reveals itself. That was the only honest way I knew how to tell it.

And so this book became more than just pages. It became an act of witnessing myself. Of naming what tried to erase me and choosing not to be erased. It became a record of the people I love and all of the mess I carry, the boy I became and the man I am still learning to be. It became my way of saying: I was here. I lived. I mattered.

If you're holding this book, thank you. Thank you for choosing to sit with these words, for meeting me here in the middle of everything. I hope something in these pages makes you feel less alone, more real, or more allowed to keep becoming in whatever way you need to. And I hope, above all, that it reminds you staying is enough.

Before You Begin

This book contains references and descriptions of:

sexual abuse, domestic violence, poverty, addiction, and suicidal ideation. It also includes themes of gender transition, grief, self-harm, and recovery.

These topics are explored with emotional honesty and detail. If something in here feels like too much, you're allowed to put it down. You're allowed to skip ahead. You're allowed to take care of yourself first.

Healing is not linear, and neither is this story.

I:
Origins

This is me before I had words for myself.

My parents,
my brothers,
the first rooms I learned to live in.

The beginning is theirs,
but it's mine too.

Shayna Ayan: A Prologue

I've been living as a man for six years now, but I haven't gone anywhere. Not really.

It's funny, I tell people that I never had *that* childhood moment I've heard time and time again from other trans people, the moment they just *knew*. Who they were, who they wanted to be, and that early sense of otherness that set them apart. I still haven't had it. Growing up I didn't insist on a different name or fight to wear boys' clothes. I didn't grow up with a clear sense of gender friction. I wore what I was told, and did what was expected of me. I didn't question any of it, because I didn't even know there was something to question, or care enough to question much at all. In a lot of ways, I passed for normal.

I was quiet, observant, withdrawn, and deeply uncomfortable. Romantic feelings didn't hit me until late adolescence, and queerness wasn't a word I associated with myself until recently. I wasn't someone who stood out, and I tried my best to blend in. Things are very different now: there's language, representation, access. The internet alone gives young folks a map that I never had. Back then, especially in the bible belt, none of this was talked about. Maybe they whispered about it behind closed doors, maybe the church sermon took a dig or two, but I didn't come from a religious household and silence was louder than any condemnation. To me, being queer meant being quiet.

I suppose the only sign that something was different about me at all was that I had a deeply rooted shame for my developing chest that I could not name. I always hated having breasts, and unfortunately for me, I was also quite *blessed* in that regard. By tenth grade I wore a 34G. As of writing this, I'm still healing from having them removed, and they took off twelve and a half pounds of tissue. Back when I started binding my chest, I didn't even know what it was that I was doing, I just knew that being flat felt good.

Donatello Dreakford

Before I had language and terms like transgender, dysphoria, or top surgery, I held a quiet and ugly fantasy I never said out loud. I prayed nightly to a god I didn't believe in and *wished for breast cancer*. I'd watch those medical dramas where a woman gets the diagnosis and melodramatically breaks down over losing her womanhood, and I'd sit there, absolutely puzzled. The sweet release of death *or* a double mastectomy sounded like a pretty good deal to me. So, maybe I didn't come across as normally as I remember.

There are days I wake up and still feel her just underneath the surface. The hurt little girl, the quiet adolescent, and the woman I stepped out of because it was the only way I knew how to keep going. People say transition is a second chance in life, and maybe it is, but for me there's never been a day where she isn't still with me somehow.

At nearly twenty years old I started hormones in secret. For months it was me, covertly watching my body shift in ways I had dreamed of but didn't yet have the courage to name out loud. Coming out wasn't a single moment. It was a hundred small calculations: when to speak, who might understand, and how much of myself I could risk showing. I told a couple of close friends almost six months later when my voice started deepening and I couldn't pass it off for anything else. I told my family a bit after that, because shirts stopped fitting and time felt thin. Each confession felt less like celebration and more like obligation, as if I had to explain myself before someone else demanded answers. I only said it out loud once it became too visible to deny, and because on some level I thought I owed them that explanation.

At twenty-one I climbed into the ashtray on wheels I called a car, left my small hometown in North Carolina, and drove west until I hit Seattle, Washington. People ask me, why Seattle? I still couldn't tell you. I think it was simply the farthest I could drive, and that was just going to have to be enough. I knew that to start anew and

3

become someone else, I had to be completely rid of my past. I would not be able to do that with all the weight I was carrying from my trauma, and all the hurt etched into my name.

It's almost like a cheat code in a way, to begin transitioning, and then just go somewhere else. To go far enough from where you began that no one knows a *before*. People accept what they see. You get to pick and choose which parts of you to keep, and which parts to let go. You become the one curating your own history. I tried to forget all of my darkest parts and rewrote the worst versions of myself one by one as I drove across the states. Far enough to bury her in silence. Something I've learned since is that silence isn't the same as healing.

Shayna Ayan.

I haven't said her name out loud in years, and I don't miss it. Still, I know and honor what it carries. There's a part of her, of me, that no one knows about. A deep truth I still carry that I haven't been able to shake loose.

The first time I learned that touch could hurt, I was five years old.

The boy across the street was just a little older than me, maybe seven or eight years old. He was my brother's friend, and he'd come over after school with jelly still stuck on his face to talk to my brothers about Power Rangers, video games, and who could beat who.

When no one was watching, he would pull me into quiet rooms and close the door behind us. He called it a game. I didn't know what that meant back then, because I thought games had rules. I thought games were supposed to be fun, something you wanted to play. I thought games ended when you said stop. This one never did.

Sometimes I remember the sound of the door more than anything else. The soft click as it latched. The muffled noise of my brothers yelling at the TV in the next room. The flick of my mother's lighter as she smoked just a few feet away on the other side of my wall. The whirring of the ceiling fan overhead, slow and steady, as if nothing was wrong at all.

I learned quickly that I was supposed to keep still and keep silent. My body understood long before my mind ever did. His hands. His tongue. The smell of peanut butter on his breath from the sandwich he ate before coming over. The way the sunlight from the wide-open window shifted across the floor as the afternoon stretched on.

It lasted over a year.

I remember one afternoon on the top bunk, my brothers sitting cross-legged on the floor below, their laughter rising and falling with the chaos of the video game on the TV. Their voices were so close, almost close enough to reach me, but it felt like they belonged to another life entirely. Another world. Above them, I stayed quiet. Pinned beneath him, the mattress dipping under both of our weight. My chest burned from holding my breath so tightly, as if breathing might give us away.

Sometimes I wonder if anyone ever knew. If there was something on my face. In the way I moved. If proof of it lived somewhere on me, visible to everyone but myself.

I think my dad sensed it, because one afternoon he pulled me aside and crouched eye level. He said if anyone ever touched me without my permission, to hit them hard. I nodded, though I did not understand why he was saying it to me right then.

The next time the boy came over, he reached for me, like always. My body shook, but my fist didn't. I swung with everything I had and felt the sharp snap of knuckles meeting bone. Blood rushed from his nose and down his lip, staining the front of his shirt. He stopped coming over, and he never touched me again.

By then, the damage was done. Not just the pain, but the questions. The way it rewired me. The silence that formed like scar tissue around my mouth

I always wonder how I'd have turned out, how I would've developed if I'd never had this strange first encounter with sexuality.

5

Man Enough for Myself

If this one sequence of experiences snowballed into everything that followed. The reason I think my feelings of the whole thing are so complex is because I wasn't molested by some evil adult. He was another child, the very same kid I went on to sit next to in eighth grade math for an entire semester. A child that from somewhere, and I've come to realize someone else probably did it to him first. Which would make him a victim, too. I've made peace with the fact that I'll probably never know for sure.

My dad was always keeping watch over me when I was young. I think, in his own way, he still is. There are so many things I survived because of him, and I will always be grateful for that. But he couldn't be everywhere. He couldn't see everything, and in the spaces where his eyes weren't, a few more slipped through the cracks.

When I was twelve years old, my dad moved out of the home to remarry, and my mother let a man stay with us. He was her friend's ex-husband. He took my room, and I was moved to the floor beside her bed, or the couch when she wanted space. I learned how to fold myself small in corners, to pretend it didn't matter where I slept. He never laid a hand on me, but I found what he left open on his computer. Videos. Children. Boys.

I showed it to my mother. She looked at me, then she looked away.

He stayed.

The man liked my baby brother too much, and I hated it. I noticed the way he pulled him into his lap just a little too often, holding him just a little too long. My stomach knotted every time, a tightness I didn't have words for back then. What gutted me most wasn't only what he did, but the thought of it reaching my brothers. I could not, under any circumstances, allow what happened to me to happen to either of them. Maybe that's why it carved so deeply, because I never valued myself enough to speak out, but when I finally found the courage to do it for my little brother, nobody cared. My mother chose a man who paid some of the bills over the safety of her children. That betrayal has always stayed louder than the rest.

So, I made myself *unbearable*. I fought with my mother over everything. Slammed doors. Broke rules on purpose. Made my presence burn hot enough to make everyone else miserable and push him out. I wanted him gone, and if no one else was going to do it, I would.

Eventually, he left.

That was the first time I became my own mother. It was also the last time I believed I had one. When people ask me why after all of these years I don't want to find her and reconnect, this is what comes to mind. Mourning the idea of a mother who protects you, who loves her children unconditionally, at such a young age. It rewires something in you, and it cannot be undone.

What happened a few years later only cemented that reality.

I was sixteen, working nights at Zaxby's, and I used to walk home along the side of Highway 55 because I had no ride. The walk was long and desolate, just two narrow lanes cutting through endless stretches of grass, trees, and almost nothing else. My mother never drove me home. Not because she couldn't, not because she had somewhere else to be, but simply because she didn't feel like it.

Sometimes I would get lucky, and my friend Vana would drive me home after our shift. But that night, she wasn't working, so I clocked out and started the walk.

About a mile in, the air felt heavy and damp, clinging to my skin. There were no streetlights, no houses, no noise except for the crunch of gravel and dead grass under my non-slip shoes and the cicadas screaming into the dark.

It was close to midnight when a pickup truck passed me. I watched the taillights get smaller and smaller until they started to disappear into the night. Then, a few hundred feet ahead, the red glow of brake headlights flared.

The truck slowed, then stopped.

Man Enough for Myself

I told myself maybe it was nothing. Maybe someone was just offering a ride.

It wasn't.

The moment it whipped around, sharp and fast, my stomach dropped. The front headlights began to come at me, bright and cold, and I couldn't see anything else. Back then, it was all highway and trees. No businesses, no houses, no traffic this late. If something happens, nobody hears you.

My brain blocks a lot of it out. What flashes still is trying to look up at the night sky as it happened. Trees whispering in the breeze, and quiet. The warm and wet sensation of hot breath on the back of my neck. The taste of grass and earth in my mouth as my face pressed into the ground, and the small chip on my front tooth that takes me back to that feeling of knowing that nobody was going to pass by and save me. Gravel scratched my knees. The stars blinked overhead. There was no one on that highway but me and him, and I never screamed. I didn't see the point of it.

When he left, I laid there on my back for a long time. Blood between my legs. Mosquitoes biting. The crickets humming like nothing had happened. The stars were so bright it almost made me laugh.

I learned this there: the world can be beautiful and not give a damn about you. The sky can be loud, and nobody comes. I carry that with me every day.

That night, I went home. Washed up. Went to bed. I never said a word to anyone. Not about the walk, not about the truck, not about the way the fear settled into my body and never really left.

Weeks later, I was pregnant. I walked into a clinic with my minimum-wage paycheck folded tight in my pocket and walked out less than I was before. Emptied. Not just of what was growing, of something I didn't know I could lose. Mine, and I only knew it after it was gone. I was a child and then I wasn't. Sometimes I wonder if I ever really got to be one at all.

Donatello Dreakford

Throughout most of my years that followed, I never dated. I never let anyone touch me. I didn't believe touch could mean anything but pain. That belief, and what came before, led me down a darker path than I knew then. Somewhere along the way, I stopped seeing my body as mine. I started seeing it the way the world had taught me to: as something to be used, not something to be loved.

Then came nineteen. By then, I'd already dropped out of school. I was living on my own, barely keeping the lights on, and I started paying rent by letting older men fuck me in motel rooms and strangers' houses.

I remember the first time too well. I stepped out of my car and walked across the cracked pavement of a parking lot slick with oil stains. My hands wouldn't stop shaking and I felt nauseous. The motel elevator smelled like sweat and bleach, metal and heat. I counted the floors without meaning to, the numbers lighting up one by one. I knocked on the door, crossed the threshold, and something in me stayed behind. It felt like crossing into a new era of my life in the worst way. No going back after that, and I didn't.

Before, my body had been taken from me, this was something different. This was me handing it over, piece by piece, because somewhere along the way I'd already given up on it.

Of course, there's nothing wrong with sex work. Nothing wrong with doing what you can to survive, but I was too young, and no one ever told me there were other ways to live.

I started stripping after that, and then I started disappearing. I learned to dissociate with style, turned myself into a spectacle so no one would look too closely. The money came fast, and the drugs came faster. I lived off alcohol, pills, and cheap cigarettes, clinging to whatever would make me numb enough to keep letting it happen. To keep showing up, night after night, pretending none of it touched me.

I don't think I ever hated sex, exactly. I just never learned it was supposed to feel good. I didn't believe I was supposed to feel good.

9

Man Enough for Myself

If I'm being honest, I still don't. Pleasure has always felt like a trap, something other people were allowed to want. For me, it was just another thing to endure. Touch became a transaction. A ritual. Something I clocked into, like a shift. Like penance. Like punishment.

And even now, at twenty-six, I don't know if I've come all the way back. I've had lovers by choice. People who've asked first. People who've wanted to know me, not just touch me. And still, I've never had sex without lying. Without acting. Without silently begging myself to stay in my body and failing every time. I've never orgasmed with another person, not once. I've never felt real desire in the moment, only the quiet need to survive it, to get through it, to not ruin things by showing too much of what I couldn't feel. Every time someone has asked me, "Was that good for you?" I've smiled. I've nodded. I've lied.

I live in this body now. Flat chested, clean shaven, and deep voiced. Hands in my pockets like armor, but too many days, I still feel like I'm looking out from behind her eyes.

The girl I used to be shows up before me in the mirror when I brush my teeth. I button shirts over the chest she once hated, the one myself and those around me spent years scraping together thousands to sculpt into mine. I walk into rooms she never made it out of. She curls up in the corners of my bed. Slips into my silence. Tugs at my memory. She shows up when someone I love touches me gently and I can't stay. She lingers in the moments I wish I could fully claim.

I don't know how to let her go, I'm not even sure if I should. Still, she got me through. She survived a life I wouldn't have, but I want something different now. Not to erase her, not to forget, but to remember without disappearing. To be held without folding. To want, and be wanted, and actually stay.

Every time I try to get close, I remember the moment I stepped out of my body. The man in the motel room. The door closing. The weight of his hands where mine should have been, and I don't know if I'll ever be able to step back in.

Or maybe it happened before that.

Maybe it was the night I lay in a ditch, laughing up at the stars because it was easier than crying.

Maybe it was when I gave up my bedroom for a stranger and stopped trusting my mother.

Or when something was taken from me before I was old enough to understand what it meant to choose.

Maybe I was already gone by then.

Maybe I never stood a chance.

Maybe it started when I was five years old.

I'll never know.

Man Enough for Myself

Donatello Dreakford

Christine

I never called her Mom.

She hated that.

I think deep down
she knew she didn't earn it.

Christine and I
were doomed from the start
because she was the kind of woman
who didn't raise daughters,
she raised rivals.

She hated my father.
Said it with her whole chest
and still had three kids with him.

They were never in love,
never even liked each other.

Yet somehow
they made a family
the same way people build houses
out of broken glass
wondering why it all keeps bleeding.

As a kid
I used to think parents had to be married
to make babies.

I would kneel at my bed
small hands clasped
and pray for a divorce,
as long as I got to go with my father.
(I didn't.)

Nothing I did was ever right.

Donatello Dreakford

Now I see it clearly,
she hated the parts of me
that reminded her of herself.

The way I walked,
the way I looked,
the way I made her remember
who she used to be.

She'd been the black sheep once, too.
She just made sure I wore it louder.

I wasn't special.
I was just my father's favorite,
and that alone was enough.

Even though they screamed
through the walls every night
and shattered the kitchen
like breaking things
was the only language they shared,
I think she loved him.

Or she wanted to keep him,
and she couldn't.

Her favorite performance
was packing a bag by the door,
rounding us up like evidence
that she mattered,
and threatening to leave.

We never went,
she just liked being watched.

Christine was tall,
loud,
face and chest spattered with freckles,

Man Enough for Myself

her skin always red
and flushed like rage
simmered just under the surface.

Hair all split ends and broken thread,
thin and angry.

The stench of Newports on her breath
spewing hate and empty promises.

She smelled like ash and drive-thrus.

So did the car,
so did our house,
so did I,
riding behind her
as the smoke blew back in my face.

She hated her own body
and made sure I hated mine.

Tried every crash diet she could afford
then cried over wrappers in her minivan.

If she wasn't starving herself,
she was starving us.

If she wasn't calling herself disgusting
she was calling me worse,
her voice sharp like a scalpel
my skin still remembers.

I learned to walk on eggshells
before I learned to tie my shoes.
Got good at not stepping wrong,
tiptoeing through the house
like I was auditioning for survival.

Donatello Dreakford

She loved my brothers.
Or at least,
she didn't hate them.

We all grew up in the same house
but lived in different worlds.

They got warmth,
I got warnings.
They got praise,
I got proof I was broken.

She called me ugly.
Unfixable.
Fucked up.

I told her once
about what they did to me,
she told me I was lying.

"Who would want *you*?"

She never let me shower alone
until middle school.
Yanked my hair,
turned the water up
so high it scalded,
said it was my fault
if I cried,
said it was my fault
for being dirty.

Took me to doctors
to prove I wasn't right,
to prove something
had to be wrong with me.

Man Enough for Myself

The doctors never found anything,
but she kept looking.

She spoke to me
like I was something stuck to her shoe.

Not a person,
just a problem
she couldn't throw away,
no matter how much she wanted to.

When she wasn't cruel
she was collapsing.

Told me she wanted to die,
that I ruined her life,
that it was my fault my dad left,
that he never wanted me,
that he'd started a new life
without us.

She said everything wrong with her
was wrong with me.
Said I'd never be anything
but a reflection of her failure.

Christine lied
like she was breathing,
not in clever ways,
just compulsively.

Said she had degrees,
then said she worked jobs.
I never saw her work
a day in my life.

She wanted trophies
and she wanted power.

Donatello Dreakford

She didn't want kids,
she wanted leverage,
child support checks,
and pity points.

She tried to paint my dad
as a threat in black skin
to win full custody.

The court believed her,
of course they did.

She was white,
crying,
alone.

He was ordered
to send money every month.
She spent it on cigarettes,
or alcohol,
or fast food,
whatever she could smoke or swallow.

We lived in filth
like vermin.
Hungry
and empty,
like our pantry.

In clothes with holes,
so she could play the victim
to anyone who would listen.

Near the end,
she slipped further.
We were just witnesses
to her slow-motion drowning.

Man Enough for Myself

She sank into a mattress on the floor,
surrounded by garbage and filth,
talking to people who weren't there.

I watched through the crack in her door
as she argued with ghosts,
and let the cigarettes burn
down her fingers
until they yellowed and shook.

When she wasn't doing that
she was screaming,
or silent,
or laughing in my face
when I tried to die.

And still,
sometimes I feel bad for her.
Not in a way that excuses it,
just enough to say
I know she was unwell.

But long before she unraveled,
she chose cruelty.
She had chances,
and never took them.

The day the police came
and my father took us away,
I never looked back.

Not out of hatred,
but because she never reached out again.
Not once.
Not to say sorry,
not to ask how I was.

Donatello Dreakford

I think she spoke to my brothers
once or twice over the years,
but never me.

Without child support
I was no longer useful.

I wasn't a daughter,
not even a memory,
just a check
that stopped clearing.

And honestly?
That didn't break me.
It freed me.

I stopped mourning a mother
who never existed,
and left Christine
right where she belonged,
in the past.

Ash in my pockets.

Dwayne

My father has always been the one who saw me
even before I saw myself.

When the world tried to tell me
he was dangerous,
a threat,
a man to fear,
I looked at him and saw
strength that didn't shrink,
kindness that didn't need softening,
and a presence that didn't apologize
for taking up space.

I knew they were wrong,
because if they were right
I would be too,
and I am not
because we are the same.

He raised me on early alarms
and clean counters.

Taught me a black man could cry at the sink,
rinse his face,
and keep going.

Could care deeply,
could hold his children
like they were something breakable.

He treats his body like a well-oiled machine.
Disciplined. Powerful. Bright.
Skin smooth as vinyl
and shaved to the scalp.

Donatello Dreakford

I've never seen him with hair,
only that clean glinting head in the sun
and a face always fresh with aftershave.

He taught me how to take care
of my own skin,
how to walk out the door
looking like you *meant to*.

Crisp jeans,
a Ralph Lauren polo,
sneakers so clean
they looked untouchable,
because he is.

A man who wears his pride
on his sleeve,
and his wrist,
with a watch to match.

His brow is stern,
but he gave me those same soft eyes,
the kind that see everything.

A big mouth,
a booming laugh,
a voice that carried,
an existence
that filled the room
before he ever had to say a word.

He never asked me to be smaller.
When I took up the whole room,
he said
let *them* make space.

Man Enough for Myself

Never flinched when I was too much,
just stayed.

When I ran,
he waited.
When I lied,
he called anyway.
He didn't always have the words
but he never needed them.

He showed up in silence,
in the steady hum of his car engine
waiting out front longer than he said he would,
in the clink of his keys at the door,
in the way the light was always on
and the food was still hot.

He never scolded,
never asked where I'd been,
just made sure there was a place for me to land
without a word about how late I was.

I was messy,
angry,
disappearing,
but he never disappeared on me.

I don't know what his childhood was like.
Not all of it.

I picture it in flashes,
a front porch in Jeannette with chipped paint,
or the echo of a belt behind a slammed door.

I wonder if he looked up to his father
the way I look up to him.
I wonder if grief caught him

Donatello Dreakford

the same way it caught me,
quiet and sudden like winter after rain.

If losing his mother made the world go still.

I imagine her in the corners of our family,
in the crease between his brows when he's focused,
in the way he folds towels just so,
in the way he loved me loud
and got sharp when I was drifting.

Other people thought he was too hard on me,
but he and I knew different.
He knew I needed someone to hold the line,
to teach me discipline without shame,
to meet my defiance with belief.

That kind of love don't come easy,
but I think he got it from her.

I never met her,
but I see her in the way
he kept showing up anyway,
even when I made it hard.

We didn't take the same path
but somehow
I ended up just like him.

Stubborn. Honest. Tired. Still standing.

I let him name me,

Donatello.

No hesitation,
no explanation,
he just said it
and I knew.

Man Enough for Myself

Not every trans person gets that.
Gets to be named by someone who saw them first.

I kept my middle name too,
because he gave me that as well.

Our initials are the same now,

D.A.D.

It makes me laugh sometimes
how even in the letters I carry,
I carry him.

Some people search their whole lives
for a model of manhood.
I was lucky enough to be raised by mine.

Not perfect,
but real.

Emotional,
whole,
and *here*.

I don't know how many times I'll get to tell him this,
but if I only get one:

Thank you, Dad.

For seeing me,
for staying,
for naming me something
I could grow into,
and for being the kind of man
I still want to become.

Donatello Dreakford

Brothers

We were raised in the same storm
but came out different.

Three kids with the same last name,
same hungry eyes,
the same bruises
in different places.

The same roof,
but the damage landed different
on each of us.

I remember the heat in that house,
how summer clung to the walls like mold,
how we learned early not to cry too loud,
not to ask for seconds,
never to flinch when the door slammed.

T was always the quiet one,
he still is.
He watched more than he spoke,
took it all in.

He had a different version of our mother than I did.
So when she left,
he didn't crumble until after.
Didn't see it coming,
didn't get to grieve her
before she was gone.

We both flunked out of the same college,
same campus,
one year apart,
one year in,
just like that.

Donatello Dreakford

We both grew up lonely,
I learned how to come out of it,
he didn't.

He's still at the house,
still under our dad's roof,
still stuck like a song on repeat
from a time I don't know how to reach anymore.

I see how bright he is,
how funny,
how lovable,
but I don't think he does.
I don't know if the world does either.

Sometimes I get scared,
because when I was in that same place,
I tried to end it all.

I wonder if he's ever thought about it too.

I hate that I think that
because if I'm honest
I don't know him like I used to,
and he doesn't know me.
Not this version.

It's strange visiting now.
He looks at me like I'm familiar,
but maybe not the same.

And maybe I'm not.

I used to be his little sister,
now I'm someone else
wearing the same memories
in a different shape.

Man Enough for Myself

Though when we laugh,
it still sounds the same.

And then there's J,
the youngest,
the golden one.

He was the mascot of our family,
the loudest,
the tallest,
the easiest to love.

Where we struggled,
he soared.
Friends.
Sports.
Good grades.

He made it onto the football team
and into a four-year university,
something neither of us managed.

For a while,
I thought he was safe.
I thought he'd made it out.

But trauma doesn't care about timing,
and hurt never waits.

T and I remember the *before*,
the warm pockets of calm
before everything got hard.
He doesn't.
His beginning started in the mess,
and I think maybe that shaped him too.
We're just seeing it now.

Donatello Dreakford

He spent his teen years with Dad,
we didn't.
We were still with *her*.

I thought that meant he got the better shot,
and maybe he did,
but even then
the hurt caught up with him too.

He went to college,
a real one,
with dorms and meal plans,
futures mapped out
on glossy brochures.

I was so sure he'd make it.
We all were,
because he was the baby,
the golden one,
the reason my dad fought so hard
to get us out.

It hurt more when he didn't make it out untouched.
Because I was always the messy one,
T was always quiet,
but J,
he was the bright one,
the one who could've made it.

And still,
by the end of his first year
he came back.
Quiet,
withdrawn,
like someone had turned the lights off inside him.

Man Enough for Myself

Just like me.
Just like T.

It was like watching history fold in on itself.

Three different boys,
same story.
Three different roads,
same crash.

I wonder sometimes
if I feel like a stranger to him now.

If my voice throws him off,
if he ever misses the sister he used to have,
or if deep down
he always knew this version of me was coming.

He's never asked questions,
never wavered,
he just passes me the remote,
lets me eat what he cooks,
lets me stay.

It's strange being their brother now
instead of their sister.

Now when I visit
we don't say much,
we don't need to.

T stays in his room mostly,
quiet like he always was.
J's taller now,
but mostly lives online.
We all eat food,
pass each other plates,

and I ask how they're doing
but not too directly.

There's a kind of love
that doesn't need a lot of words,
the kind that just
makes sure your name is still saved in your phone
and still answers on the second ring.

I wonder if they know
how much I think about them,
how often I want to go back
and start it all over,
give them both a different kind of beginning.

But we've never talked like that.

Instead,
I just stay a little longer,
make sure they eat,
tell a joke,
leave the light on.

Still,
they're mine
and I'm theirs.

We don't ever say it.
We don't have to,
it's in the silence,
the ride,
the eye contact that says
I got you
without saying a word.

Man Enough for Myself

There's a kind of love between brothers
that doesn't ask for performance,
that doesn't need proving.

It just is,
and it stays.

Even after everything.

II:
Between Names

This is me trying to figure out who I was.

Between the body I was given
and the one I made myself.

Between a voice that broke
and a voice that carried.

Buried

I used to count them like prayers.

Little white bricks of silence
lined up on the table,
each one promising less of me.

I'd swallow until the hours
slid off their hinges,
morning turned to midnight
and back again
without ever showing its face.

I lost whole days like loose change,
checked my pockets
and came up empty.

My tongue chalked over
my chest on autopilot,
my body doing the work of living
while my mind crawled into a corner.

I called it comfort,
I called it survival.

Really it was just forgetting,
pill after pill,
until forgetting was all I knew.

You see,
forgetting has always been easier
than remembering.

I woke in strangers' rooms,
on bathroom floors,
at work,
behind the wheel,

or behind my own eyes
without knowing the week.

People told me their stories
like we had lived them together,
and I nodded,
because maybe we had.

I was never there to remember.

I wanted nothing,
that was the whole point.
To be blank enough to float,
and small enough to vanish.

And still,
I kept coming back,
mouth open like a wound,
hands shaking for the next pill
that would push me under
just long enough
to forget I was drowning.

I dug the hole deeper
because it felt like home.
Since the dark was softer
than the mirror's glare.
Because I didn't love myself enough
to climb out.

I stayed buried,
piling earth over my own chest,
a shovel in one hand
and pills in the other.
Each swallow
another scoop of grit
tossed over my own place in the ground.

Man Enough for Myself

My breath shallow as an unmarked grave,
skin graying at the edges,
fingers trembling for the next collapse.

The deeper I went,
the quieter it got.
My heartbeat muffled
and my thoughts pressed flat.

Each swallow another layer
pressed over my own face.

I dreamed of air
but never reached for it.
The weight above me felt easier
than lifting my arms.

Down there,
there was no light to betray me.
The earth did not resist me,
it opened.
It welcomed.
It swallowed me whole,
bone by bone,
until I was nothing but a hollow
carved in the shape of a person
who never learned how to stay.

I knew only the comfort of sinking,
further and further,
lungs collapsing inward,
heartbeat fading to a whisper,
thoughts dimming to static
until even the silence
grew heavy enough to crush me.

Donatello Dreakford

Still,
I sank.

Soil in my mouth,
soil in my chest,
soil in the spaces where love
was supposed to live.

I sank
until there was no difference
between the body and the earth,
between the grave and the bed,
between living and not.

I sank
until nothing was left
but the weight of wanting
to never rise again.

Brown Paper Bag

I picked up the vials,
the needles,
the tiny alcohol swabs
and stowed them away
for a week.

Not because I didn't want it,
I wanted it so badly I thought
my skin would split
if I waited longer.

The point of no return
sitting in a brown paper bag.

A body you cannot hide.
A life you cannot pretend didn't happen.

They say hormones save lives,
and they did.

Saving me meant opening me all the way.
The smell of alcohol on my thigh,
the pinch,
the plunger,
my hands shaking like I was signing a contract
with my own blood.

After that,
everything started happening in public.

My face sprouted hairs
I could not shave fast enough.

My voice dropped in uneven steps
like a child
learning to walk in the dark.

Donatello Dreakford

Cashiers noticed,
friends noticed,
coworkers heard my name
moving to a lower floor.

I was expected to be a fully formed adult
while I was still unfolding.

Awkward.
Silly, even.

Unserious in a way
that made me laugh at myself
and keep going.

I built thick skin because I had to.
Palms toughening,
shirts shrinking across shoulders,
new hairs waking everywhere
like sprouts breaking soil.

The barber took so much weight off my head
I looked like myself for the first time,
and also like a stranger I trusted.

I learned tricks no one taught me.

Looser pants,
belt one notch wider,
wear them lower on the waist
because my center of gravity shifted,
and that's where comfort lives now.

Stand with weight in the heels,
let the hips be quiet,
hands in pockets when they want to be,
and look ahead
as if you already know the way.

Man Enough for Myself

My voice kept dropping,
and confidence finished the job.

I speak deeper because I believe in myself.
Self-assuredness carries its own volume.

Clarity sits in the chest,
and the throat makes room.

People hear certainty
and stop squinting at your edges.

At first,
I wanted everything
they said a man should have.

Muscle.
Square jaw.
Deep voice.
Broad chest.

I measured myself
against pictures I did not love,
counted hairs,
listened for gravel,
wished for a map someone else drew.

Over time I learned manhood
is a room you build,
walls set at the angle
you can breathe in.

I let go of that checklist,
and almost immediately
my body handed me half of it anyway.

Like it had been waiting for me
to know who I was,
to drop the costume

before offering the changes
I thought I needed.

There is no science to that,
only the way it felt.

My body wanting proof I could hold myself
before it set the voice lower
and widened the doorframes.

If you are reading this
and waiting a week with the brown paper bag
tucked in the cupboard,
I know that room.

Rest your hand.
Take the shot when you are ready.

Do the inside work even when no one can see it.
Wear your pants where comfort tells you to.
Speak from the place that tells the truth.
Walk like you belong, because you do.

By two years in,
I caught my reflection laughing.

I saw my dad in the shape of my hands,
my brothers in the angle of my shoulders,
little echoes in the jaw when I smile.

I wanted to be a man.

Six years in,
I became myself.

That is better.

Becoming

I put myself out there one day,
shaky hands,
flat chest,
still learning how to breathe
in this new architecture of myself.

My nerves fluttered
like I was fifteen again,
standing in front of someone
in a shirt that finally fits.

My new chest
still baby-soft with hope,
this was *adolescence,*
but gentler this time.

Still,
some part of me
didn't believe I could be wanted.

How could someone want this?
Want me?
See beauty in a frame
I am still meeting in the mirror?

They did.

Told me I was attractive,
touched my arm like they meant it,
invited me into the yes,
the now,
the let's go.

And *god,*
I wanted it.

Donatello Dreakford

Desperate,
feral,
hungry for affection
like a first slow dance
in a suit that was never mine.

But my hands couldn't reach back,
my lips stitched themselves shut
holding back all the ways
I wanted to say:

Yes.
Yes.
Yes.

I sat in my room hours later,
alone,
pressing questions into the silence.

Why couldn't I open my mouth
and say what I meant?

Then,
a quiet knowing.

It wasn't fear,
wasn't shame,
wasn't even uncertainty.

It was *protection.*

My body,
newly mine,
finally worthy.

For the first time
I wanted to shield it,
honor it,
wait for the hands that ask permission

Man Enough for Myself

not just with words,
but with presence.

Presence that feels soft,
untried
like a first touch,
reading my silence
not rushing
just waiting
as though my body is an offering still unfolding.

Not in words,
but in how they are with me.
Tender,
shy,
as if this were the first time.

And maybe,
just maybe
that hand should be mine first.

So yes
I want the touch,
the wanting,
but more than anything
I want to keep this sacred body safe
just a little longer.

Because now I know:

It's worthy.
It's mine.
It's love.

5'2

I'm so tired of insecure little white boys
from the pacific northwest
squeaking up at me
from somewhere around my clavicle,
telling me I'm not *man enough*
while tiptoeing in Doc Martens
two sizes too big.

I look down,
and all I see is
dry,
exposed,
scalp.

Nobody told them to take finasteride
before hopping on hormones
and now their hairline's running
faster than they can cry
about being oppressed.

In sneakers,
I'm their ceiling.
In heels?
They're a rumor I can't confirm
without my glasses on.

I could step on them,
but I have arch support
and self-respect.

I don't bend for boys
who couldn't survive a real summer,
let alone a southern one.

Donatello Dreakford

I'm not just any man,
I'm a southern-born,
strong-backed,
daddy-loved,
black transgender man
who's seen more in a year
than they will in their entire
short little lives.
(Literally, short.)

I made manhood mine.
Cut it clean.
Held it steady.

Wore it soft or sharp
depending on the day.
They hate that I didn't beg for it.
It just came to me.

They hate that I'm free,
that I've got a family back home
who call me
"he"
with pride in their voices,
and a dad who brags about his *son*
like I'm the best decision he ever made.

They're still begging their parents
to stop deadnaming them at Christmas,
while my dad loved me enough
to give me my name.

Not the one I was born with,
the one I rose into,
and said it like he'd been waiting
my whole life to say it.

Man Enough for Myself

Maybe that's why they can't stand me,
their manhood is store bought
and mine's hand carved.

They puff their chests
like men raised on Wi-Fi,
and talk slick
like I wasn't raised in heat,
in hush,
in hurricane.

They walk into rooms unnoticed,
still chasing "passing" like a prize.

When I walk in
the air changes
because I don't pass,
I arrive.

They confuse loud for strong,
mean for confident,
and passing for real.

But let me make one thing clear:
Transition is not a competition.

The second you start competing,
you've already lost.

Especially when you try to compete with me,
if you're going to try
you'd need a ladder
just to reach my level,
and even then
you'd still be looking up.

Probably Just Vers

There's a hunger living in me
with no face,
no name,
no shape.

Just heat.

Just ache.

A thrum beneath my skin,
aching with want
without knowing what for.

Sometimes I want to be held down,
fragile,
soft,
like prey,
trembling under the weight of want.

Handled slowly,
bitten,
not kissed.
Split open like something ripe,
leaking,
used sweetly,
claimed like a body meant for offering.

Other times I want to hold someone down,
steady,
sharp,
like a predator,
teeth bared in the shape of a smile.

To grip them hard,
watch them beg,
opened like a mouth made for me.

Donatello Dreakford

Taken roughly,
kept like a secret
I refuse to share.

I shift.
I shimmer.

Some days I ache like a girl,
others I pulse like a man.

I want them all,
the sharp edges of masculinity,
the aching curves of femininity.
I want hands with calluses
and mouths painted in gloss.

I want to be undone
and to be the undoing.

But mostly,
I imagine.

I play these scenes
in the theater of my skull,
body pressed to body,
breaths tangled,
names whispered
like confessions.

And I wonder
if any of it is real.

If anyone truly touches
this deeply,
with this much hunger,
that much reverence.

Because I *don't* know,
I haven't lived it.

Man Enough for Myself

I feel like a fraud,
hungry for things
I've never tasted.

Shame hums in the silence
after every fantasy,
because I don't know,
because I want it all,
even if I never touch it.

Donatello Dreakford

Liked

This morning
I woke with that quiet weight again.

That feeling
that I am unworthy of love,
even though logically
I know I am.
(Or at least, I hope I am.)

For years
I stayed silent,
afraid to reach,
to risk,
to want.

How could anyone like me
when I've never learned to like myself?

I say I love me,
and I do.
(Or at least, I try to.)

But I don't like me.
Not enough to believe
someone else could.

I give myself to people
who say they love me,
but never say they see me.
People who don't like me either,
just like I don't.
People who take what they want,
and leave me holding the pieces.

It's what I know,
what I think I deserve,

Donatello Dreakford

what keeps choosing me
when the ones who would be gentle
never reach back.

My friends say I'm crazy.
They see something in me,
something bright,
something worthy.

How can I believe them
when every hand that's ever touched me
taught me to flinch?

How do you unlearn the truth
your body has memorized?

How do you stop reaching
for the only kind of love
that has ever reached for you?

The kind of love that leaves bruises
where hands once were?

The kind of love
that carved its shape
into me.

Not gently,
but deep.

I've made peace with being the
caretaker,
brother,
son,
friend.
That's enough most days.
(Or at least, it has to be.)

Man Enough for Myself

I pour into others,
like maybe
I'll feel full too.

I stay busy,
I stay needed,
I stay far enough away
from wanting too much.

Still,
some nights
I ache to be wanted.

Not for what I offer,
nor for what I fix,
just for existing.

I want to be touched
like I'm not an apology.

Held like I belong in someone's arms,
not by accident,
not out of need,
but because they want me there.

I've only ever known
hands that take
without asking.

Touch that echoes the way
I've come to see myself,
as something to endure
not something to cherish.

So,
I stopped reaching.
Let myself believe
this is all I get.

Donatello Dreakford

And maybe it is.

Maybe the closest I'll come
to that kind of love
is writing poems about it.

Still,
I wonder what it's like
to be loved
and liked
at the same time.

Letters Home

There's a particular kind of heartbreak
that blooms with age.

When the friends you once loved the most
found shelter in places you couldn't reach,
building lives that no longer held space for you.
(And you tell yourself, that's okay.)

Maybe they fell in love.
Maybe they found people who understand them better.
Maybe they started families.
Maybe you both changed.

Or maybe like me
you moved three thousand miles away,
folded your feelings into envelopes
and prayed that love,
like a letter,
might still find its way
even if no one's home to receive it.
(It didn't.)

There is no grief quite like mourning the living.

Leaving the porch light on
for strangers who never stay,
every new connection
a pale imitation of the old warmth you lost.

How slowly your heart breaks
when the home you once clung to
inside them
gets filled by others,
and all you can do is stand outside,
nose to the glass of a window,

watching a life you once lived
move on without you.

You want to be happy for them.
(And in so many ways, you are.)

Yet happiness doesn't keep you warm
when your breath still fogs the glass
of a house you no longer have the key to.

Maybe,
I'm just lonely.

Maybe,
I need to stop writing letters
I already know will never be answered.

Man Enough for Myself

III:
The Family I Built

This is how I learned I wasn't alone.
My daughter,
my best friend,
my sister.

The people I chose
who chose me back.

Angel

The first time I saw her
was at runway training.

Fluorescent lights humming overhead,
mirrors lining the wall
like quiet witnesses.

She stood toward the back
bright-eyed,
almost hiding,
watching every movement
like it was her way forward.

Her eyes were big and waiting,
like she already knew
she belonged to something bigger.

I was 23 then,
the age she is now.

She came up to me shyly,
tucked behind a goatee and short hair
that didn't suit her softness.

"Your walk is ovah,"
she said.

Just like that,
I saw her.

The velvet in her movement,
the light beneath her voice,
she hadn't bloomed yet
but you could see the petals aching open.

Her name is Angel,
and she is.

Donatello Dreakford

Heaven-sent,
not just in name,
in every careful
powerful way
she exists in this world.

She asked me to be her *mother*
one afternoon in the park.

I laughed at first,
said no,
not because I didn't want to,
but because in our world
mother means more
than just a mentor.

It means blood
made without biology.
It means forever.
It means building family
when yours is taken too soon.

That day
she had just told me about her brother,
how she had just lost him back in Puerto Rico,
and how close they had been.

Suddenly,
her question wasn't small at all.
It was sacred.
It was everything.

Of course,
I said yes.
because some things are sacred
long before they're spoken aloud.

Man Enough for Myself

She was the first.
She is the only.

I saw her perform for the first time
in the same dive bar basement
where I first stumbled through my own drag debut,
where I tried not to choke
on the nerves and noise.

But when she stepped on stage,
all silk and shadow,
hips like question marks,
eyes like warning,
I cried.

She was performing a tribute to her brother.
Nobody else in the room knew,
but I did.

When she pulled out the framed funeral portrait,
the air shifted.
She was grieving in front of strangers,
and turning sorrow into art.

She performed *La Gata Bajo la Lluvia*.
I don't speak Spanish,
but I looked up the words later
and this part stayed with me,

"I'll be the cat under the rain
and I'll leave,
but I'll still love you."

She didn't just perform,
she *became* the song.
A woman in mourning

refusing to stop loving
just because the world told her to.

In that moment
I didn't just see her,
I recognized her.

She performs as *Gata*,
catlike and composed,
moving through smoke like a secret.

She doesn't just vogue,
she prowls.
Every gesture velveted,
every glance a dare.

Beneath the sultry spell
is someone pure hearted.
She dreams of peace,
of love that's quiet and real,
of choosing someone who chooses her back.

I warn her gently
about men who are too old,
too cruel,
too fluent in the language of control.

Because when you're young,
and still gathering the bones of yourself,
sometimes you confuse being *wanted*
with being *safe*.

But it's not.
And she deserves more.

More than survival,
more than proximity to love.

Man Enough for Myself

When she asked me to be her mother,
I was afraid.
Not of loving her,
but of not knowing how.

I have never had that kind of love.
Never felt it.

Motherhood was never in the script
for someone like me,
not in the way they wrote boyhood.

I wasn't made to nurture,
I was supposed to bury the softness deep.

I mothered myself in motel mirrors,
with split lips
and knuckles chewed raw,
whispering bedtime
into the cracks of my own chest.

I learned to hum comfort
without a blueprint,
to braid survival into softness
with hands no one taught me to use gently.

And in loving her,
this brilliant
blooming girl,
I am healing something
I didn't know was still broken.

I am showing the little girl in me
what a good mother looks like.

And *she* smiles,
not because she's finally seen,
but because she's finally *believed.*

Donatello Dreakford

Because somehow,
the man I became
learned how to love like this.

And we are both
finally safe.

About Nate

Before I knew anything about who I was, before I had the language for transness, the tools to name my grief, or the courage to imagine a life outside of survival, I met Nate. And somehow, he just... got it. We weren't in love. Not like that. We were something quieter. Queerer. Something more complicated and more sacred than most people know how to name. He wasn't my boyfriend. He wasn't even my best friend in the traditional sense. The term "best friend" doesn't feel like enough. He was my person. I still feel like he is. My mirror. My tether to the world when I was barely holding onto it.

We met when I was still going by the wrong name, still wearing a female uniform that didn't fit, still trying to be someone tolerable enough to keep around. I was all sharp corners and open wounds, and he was soft in ways I didn't trust yet: tender, observant, calm like a body of water you don't realize is deep until you're already in it. We worked together at a restaurant. We orbited each other for weeks before saying more than five words, but once we did, it was over. We were in it. The kind of friendship that makes you feel like maybe you were supposed to find each other in this lifetime.

This section is about that kind of friendship, but it's also about the messy parts. The selfish parts. The things I did that I wish I could take back. The ways in which I dragged him into my wreckage, thinking that was the same thing as intimacy, and the way he forgave me anyway. Quietly, without performance. Without conditions. Just like he always had.

We didn't say "I love you" back then. Not because it wasn't true, but because we didn't need to. It was in the shared playlists, the cigarettes, and the silence between us. Years have passed, and we don't talk much anymore. But there's a part of me that still aches from missing him. Still wants to sit in the passenger seat of his Chevy Malibu and just be near him, even if we don't say anything at all.

Donatello Dreakford

Even from across the country, he's with me. In every line I write. In every vow I've kept. In every part of me that believes people can be forgiven, loved, and seen without having to earn it.

This next section is not a story about romance. It's a story about queer friendship. About finding someone who feels like a soulmate without ever needing to kiss them. About learning how to love platonically with your whole chest, with all your flaws showing, with no roadmap, because someone showed you how.

This is for Nate. For the version of me he helped carry. For the fact that he stayed, even when I gave him every reason not to. This section is not just memory, it's an offering. A thank you. A record of what it means to be held by someone who doesn't want anything from you but for you to be okay.

It's a reminder that some of the deepest loves of our lives don't come in romantic shapes. Some arrive just when you need them most, and stay with you, even when they're no longer there.

I: The Tunnel

I spent weeks trying to speak to you.

Just a shy hostess
watching a lanky waiter
with piano fingers
and Marlboro breath
carry trays through the dining room
like it was his stage.

You had long lashes
and a laugh I wanted to memorize.

I didn't know then
why my chest ached around you,
I just knew I liked it.
Liked *you*.

The night we finally hung out
we drove to the tunnel
beneath NC State
armed with cheap spray paint
and things we didn't know how to say out loud.

We wrote our names on the wall
like we were carving initials into a tree:
"N + D"
in crooked letters.

A memory still living in a picture frame by my bed,
my favorite proof
that we existed.

Afterwards we wandered
through shuttered streets
where everything closes by ten,
talked until three in the morning on a park bench

Donatello Dreakford

about music,
fame,
pain,
the families we ran from,
and the selves we hadn't become yet.

I remember the quiet.

The kind that only happens
when you're completely seen.

You said something about how
you thought people like us
don't get happy endings.

I said maybe they do,
if we stick together
and make them for each other.

And that night
in the tunnel,
and on the bench,
we did.

II: Your Room

I always found reasons to sleep over.

After nights out at *Legends*,
after matching restaurant shifts,
late night car confessionals,
after nothing at all.

Your room was always clean,
crisp white sheets tucked tight
like a hotel bed,
the faintest smell of detergent and cologne
lingering in the air.

Nothing else but a small TV,
a few carefully placed instruments,
a closet,
and a bathroom so spotless
it made me feel like I didn't belong in it.

Still, you made space for me.
Never minded the mascara stains I'd leave on your pillow,
or the way my bag always spilled open on the floor.
You'd hand me a pair of socks and say,
"you're good"
and I believed you.

Sometimes I'd wake up
to the sound of your piano or cello
softly bouncing around the walls,
just warm enough to keep me tethered
but never loud enough to wake me.

You played like you were praying,
and I listened like it might save me.

Donatello Dreakford

We wrote music in the closet sometimes.
I curled up with a notebook,
you hunched over a keyboard
with your hoodie pulled tight.

We didn't call it sacred,
but it was.

Everything about you was tidy,
but never cold.

Everything about me was fraying at the edges,
but you never looked away.

No one had ever made space for me like that,
not without asking for something in return,
and in that quiet white room
I started to believe
maybe I was worth keeping around.

Those nights in your room bled into others.

Weeknights we went to *Legends*
just to smoke,
loiter,
and pretend we belonged
to the neon hum of the place.

You'd win every time you convinced me to play pool,
which isn't the feat you always made it out to be.

I cheered you on too loudly,
half drunk on the illusion
that we were legends
just for being there,
alive and together,
aching in our own gentle ways.

Man Enough for Myself

No one could've known
that the real story wasn't on the dance floor,
or in your quiet white room,
but in the way we leaned against each other
outside at midnight.

Two kids in borrowed shoes
laughing at nothing
and choosing each other,
time after time,
without ever needing to say it out loud.

III: Camel Crushes & Marlboro 100s

You,
a Marlboro.

Clean cut,
classic,
no filter in your words
or the way you carried pain.

Smoke sharp and dry,
tobacco curling from your lips,
proud to hurt
like you were.

Lighting up with quick certainty,
always three clicks of the lighter,
always tilted just right between your fingers
like it belonged there.

Me,
a Camel Crush.
Menthol bead tucked beneath my thumb,
waiting to crack it
like a secret I wasn't ready to tell.

No edge in my smoke,
just cool sweetness on the inhale,
a cigarette pretending to be gentle
like I was pretending to be okay.

Lighting up slow,
dragging it out,
one flick,
two hesitations,

Man Enough for Myself

holding it like maybe this time
it might steady me.

Yours was a burn you leaned into.
Mine was a mask I held between my lips.

We smoked side by side
like it meant something,
and maybe it did.

We'd end up next to each other
on curbs and car seats,
leaning into the silence
as if it had something to tell us.

Smoke rising slowly between us,
yours a straight line to the sky,
mine swirling in shapes I never learned to name.

We'd trade brands sometimes,
and laugh at how wrong they tasted
in each other's mouths.

Still,
we passed them back and forth
like it meant something.

As if understanding came
in the way you flicked ash,
and I watched it fall,
never knowing how to explain
the fire I carried
under all that menthol.

You were honest burn,
I was sugar over rot.

But in our lungs
we carried the same smoke,

Donatello Dreakford

and maybe
sharing the worst parts of ourselves
was the closest thing to love
either of us could offer back then.

IV: Passenger Seat Confession

We always felt safest in cars.

We parked in the lot
outside of your apartment,
windows fogged,
music low,
our secrets swirling
in the smoke between us.

Both of us tired,
a little spun out,
chasing that sweet quiet night's sleep
that comes after a particularly reckless evening.

This one wasn't safe.
This night was a cliff.

You asked me for one of my pills,
just one.

I should've said no,
even in the wreck of my own making,
I paused.

But then,
I gave it to you anyway.

That little blue door
to the hollow I lived in.

I don't know if I wanted to share my pain,
or if I just wanted someone to sit in it with me.
I think I mistook that kind of invitation for love.

Donatello Dreakford

You took it with a swig of my half flat Diet Coke,
talked about going to bed,
maybe grabbing a chocolate bar from the grocery store.

I told you,
don't drive, please.

As if I had any right,
like I hadn't veered off the road
more nights than I could count.

A few hours later in my bed,
my phone lit up.

A text from you,
mostly gibberish,
then:

hospital.

You'd driven anyway.

Nodded off behind the wheel
on the way to Harris Teeter
for that fucking candy bar.

You woke up in your own driver's seat
to blue lights,
broken glass,
the sound of your life rerouting
because I handed you something
you never should've held.

You could have died,
but you didn't,
and I've thanked the stars
every day since.

Man Enough for Myself

You got the DUI,
the record,
the revoked license,
the ruined plans,
the return to your parents' house
like a punishment for trusting me.

You were set to start over
back by the beach,
in a hometown you'd tried to leave behind.

And me?
I walked away untouched.

No flashing lights,
no citation,
just *shame*
so heavy
it bends my spine.

I stared at my reflection that night,
and couldn't recognize who I'd become.

How far I'd fallen,
how much damage I could cause
just by being who I was.

That night,
I flushed the rest of them down the toilet,
laid in my bed
sweating through clothes,
shaking,
vomiting,
telling my dad I had the flu.

Really,
I was grieving.

Donatello Dreakford

Not the pills,
not even the life I'd been trying to escape.

I was grieving the version of you
that still saw me as safe.

I spent a week
camped out with my phone in hand,
waiting for a message from you
saying you hated me.

It never came.

Instead,
you gave me a notebook
with a rose painted on the front,
and a letter inside
telling me it wasn't my fault.

But it was,
and it is.

That was the night
I became someone else.

The night I swore:
Never again.
Not with you.
Not with anyone.

I've kept that vow
every day since.

Not because I deserve forgiveness,
but because you gave me love
when you should've given me silence.

V: The Notebook

It should've ended there
with the flashing lights,
the slammed door,
the silence.

But he didn't vanish,
didn't curse my name,
or send back all the clothes I left at his place.

Instead,
on his last night before the move
he handed me a notebook.

Painted a pink rose on the front,
delicate as if he still saw beauty in my hands.

Tucked a letter inside the cover,
and said none of it was my fault.

I read that page over and over
until the ink blurred,
until the guilt soaked deeper
than the pills ever did.

I've carried that notebook
through several years
and several states.

I wrote poems in it when I couldn't speak aloud,
letters to you I'll never send,
journal entries that collapse
into apologies.

It's the heaviest thing I own.

Not because of the paper,
but because someone once looked at me,

at everything I had broken,
and didn't flinch.

He gave me that book
like it was nothing,
like forgiveness was easy.

I've spent years
trying to be the kind of person
who could be worthy of it.

I owe him my sobriety,
my second chance,
my entire idea of love.

Not the romantic kind,
but the kind that sees you
at your worst
and doesn't leave.

I keep the notebook where I can see it.

Not as proof of who I was,
but a reminder
of what he saw in me
when I couldn't see anything at all.

VI: After Everything

I live three thousand miles away now,
a new name,
a new body,
a new self,
learning how to be loved
without hiding.

But some days I'm still nineteen
in the parking lot of the restaurant,
watching you roll silverware in the corner
laughing at something I wish I'd heard,
heart in my throat like it always was
when I looked at you for too long.

No one here knows you,
but they all hear about you.

My beautiful friend *Nate* back home.

My twin flame in a Thrasher sweatshirt
still working at that same little wine bar,
pulling espresso shots
and charming tips out of strangers
with that soft voiced sweetness
you never turn off.

I saw you last summer,
and for a moment
it was like nothing broke.

Like the years hadn't scattered us.

We walked around like we always used to,
like our steps still matched.

Donatello Dreakford

When I had to leave,
I smiled a little too big
and held you a little too long.

It hurt more than it healed,
I came home lonelier than I'd felt in years.

I met your boyfriend last summer, too.

You brought him to the park
and he seemed kind.

I didn't notice anything wrong,
but I wonder if you did
because you broke up not long after.

Said something about
how he didn't like *me* much,
like that should matter.

You got back together
a few months later.

I saw it through photos
and scarce text messages,
the same way I catch your life now,
in little glimpses.

You haven't written back in a while,
but we haven't lost each other completely.

Not yet.

You haven't answered my latest letters,
the ones where I asked
if you were okay,
if you were happy,
if he is kind.

Man Enough for Myself

I wonder if you keep the letters
I still send.

The ink gets neater with each year,
and the stories a little brighter.

They all say the same thing,
I'm still trying to be someone
you'd be proud to know.

Even now,
even still.

The truth is,
all this growing up,
all this healing,
I didn't just do it for me.

I did it for you.

To prove that I could,
to become someone worthy
of your forgiveness,
even if you never asked me to be.

And maybe now,
you've moved on.

Maybe you love yourself
enough to never let someone
like the old me too close again.

I hope so.
God, I hope so.

Even so,
I still write you
like you might answer.

Donatello Dreakford

I still check your city's weather
like we live in the same time zone.

I still dream of you sometimes,
not of how we were,
but who we became
after everything.

And if we drift apart
for the rest of our forever,
I'll hold that younger version of us
the same way you loved me.

Tenderly.
Fully.
Like something precious
even when it's breaking.

Pixie

You showed up at nineteen
like the world had already closed the door on you,
and then you stayed.

Not my daughter,
not blood,
but kin built out of breath
and the small work of living.

I learned a kind of mother
in the way I kept the light on.
You learned a kind of home
in the way you trusted me to sleep.

You taught yourself to vogue in a garage,
no teacher,
no crowd,
just a dusty floor in Wenatchee
and a phone speaker
that kept time with your hands.

You practiced until the moves were part of your bones,
until your feet could hold stages open for you.

They call you one of the west coast's best,
I watched the hours stack up,
I kept the receipts in my head,
I watched you become
what you made yourself to be.

Remember that tiny studio we shared?
Two years pressed together
like we were trying to stop the city from getting in.

You at the flat top in the park at 2 a.m.
snapping the air into form,

me side by side with you
stomping my runway into the concrete.

We ate cheap food,
laughed too loud for the night,
then came home sore and breathless,
slept in halves still feeling whole.

Your presence filled the rooms
I did not know were empty.
When you were there
the apartment stopped feeling like a holding cell.

You were one of the first
to call me brother
and mean it.

You said it soft so it would stick.

You act hard in public,
put your face on like armor,
but behind closed doors
you let the crying come.

You missed the family that left you out.
Men break you in ways that do not make sense.

You let me see that softness,
and I hold it like a secret.

You give me the honest parts,
and I learn how to hold them steady.

You saved me more times than you know,
not with big rescues,
with small stubborn things.

Man Enough for Myself

A laugh in the kitchen when the room was grey.
A text at three a.m. that said come over.
Your shoulder when I could not find mine.

You were constant when everything else changed.

You looked at me like I mattered
even when I felt like trash,
and because you did,
I wanted to try.

Not to be clean,
not to be fixed,
just to be less of a wreck for you.

Sometimes I dream of a house
big enough to keep us both,
rooms that do not echo loneliness,
a porch that knows our names.

I picture your laundry in the dryer,
your practice videos on the TV,
and a spare bed that is already yours.

I miss the small company of you in the house,
the comfort of your shape in the room.
If I had that house,
I would leave the kitchen light on for you every night.

We are both boys who learned to be other things,
but I will always call you sister
because the word fits in my mouth like truth.

It is not a label,
it is the shape of us holding each other up.

You are stubborn,
rude,

Donatello Dreakford

funny,
and kind.

You are the tether that keeps me
from floating off into nothing.
You pull me back the way I pull you,
again and again,
because we know how to do the work.

You are not mine to save,
you are whole even when you do not know it,
and you keep me steady in ways I cannot explain.

You give me reasons to stay,
when leaving feels easier.

You look at me with that stubborn faith,
and I try because of you.

We taught each other to survive,
you taught me to keep moving
by watching you practice.

You trusted me with your true self,
and by trusting me you kept me alive

I will say it until it is true for both of us,
you are my sister.

You are the home I did not know I needed.

You kept me,
and I will keep you back.

Man Enough for Myself

IV:
Lessons in Love

This is what it looks like
to want too much.

First dates,
fast words,
the kind of love that hurt,
and the kind that finally didn't.

Too Soon

Everyone I've ever dated
said "I love you"
on our first day.

Not in bed,
not in passing,
with clear eyes and full intention
the moment after I'd asked for slowness,
for exclusivity,
for something that could last.

I *used* to think that meant I was rare.

Now I wonder if it just means
I'm easy to make a home in.

Soft walls,
and no foundation.

It's never on the first date,
never when I expect it,
but always too soon.

Right when I let myself hope.

I've studied the signs,
taken every precaution,
practiced boundaries
like I'm still trying
to believe in them,
and still,
it happened again.

I start sleeping at their place
more than my own.

Donatello Dreakford

I start rearranging the furniture
of my future
to make room for them.

Start shrinking
just a little
when they raise their voice,
even though I swore
I'd never do that again.

Even though I know
it's not my fault.

A confession
instead of a question.

A red flag
folded into a bouquet,
and I smile,
because part of me wants
so badly
to believe that this time
it's real.

That this
"I love you"
won't rot into
"I hate you"
by the first anniversary.

That I won't wake up
wondering how something
that started with softness
could end with screaming.

Even now
with all my caution,

Man Enough for Myself

all my scars lined up
like reference letters,
I still open the door
like its home
and not the scene of every crime.

Because what if I'm wrong
just *once*?

What if this is the time
they *mean it?*

What if love doesn't *have* to
leave bruises on its way in?

What if I don't have to brace for the ending?

I know how the story goes.

Even so,
I crack the window
and let the light in,
just in case.

Just this once.
Just *maybe*.

Donatello Dreakford

Exes

I watch couples unravel on TV
just to stick my nose up
and lie,
I would never put up with that.

But,
I would.

Because,
I have.

I know myself now.

I keep love at arm's length,
but if the choice is
a warm body beside me
or
being alone with the truth,
I'll take the lie.

I've done it before.

I didn't love him,
not once.

Maybe that's why
I let him get away with so much.

I let him belittle me in public,
barricade doors,
whisper threats of death
like a promise
he hoped I'd keep for him.

I never believed him,
but I stayed
and that's the worst part.

Donatello Dreakford

Because I wanted
to feel *something*.

Even misery,
even him.

He looked at me like I was magic,
I looked at him like a placeholder.

I thought I was invincible
because I didn't love him,
but even the unloved can bleed.

I've seen the others he scarred before me,
befriended them,
sat in their living rooms
to see the self-help books still left behind
like tombstones on their shelves,
heard the prayers they whispered
trying to fix
a boy who never wanted healing.

He watched me rise
and mistook proximity for credit,
thought that cheering me on
meant I belonged to him.

I carved every inch of this path myself,
he only watched.

I was young,
starving for story,
and he was just the first to say yes.

I'm grateful,
but I owe him nothing.

So, this is all he gets,
the truth.

Man Enough for Myself

He'll read this,
if he's smart.
If he's still watching,
and he'll think it means he mattered.

The truth is
that I lied
when I said I loved him.

That I stayed
when I knew better.

That I faked it
and paid the price.

Nothing beautiful in my life
came from his presence.

But I'm not angry,
and that still surprises me.

I hope someone loves him for real.
I hope he doesn't scare them.

I hope he learns
that people are not puppets,
and love is not a weapon
to wave when you're afraid
of being left behind.

I hope he stops performing
his own unworthiness.

Self-hate isn't absolution,
It's just another mask
he refuses to take off.

Donatello Dreakford

He's not so bad,
but he made himself smaller
so I'd feel guilty leaving.

And I'm not so good.

I stayed when I should've walked,
pretended to feel guilty,
and lied when I should've let go.

We weren't kids,
we were lonely,
calculated,
and dangerous in our need.

We knew better,
but we wanted more.

Even if it hurt.
Even if it broke.

And it did.

First Date

I had my very first, first date today.
I've never asked someone out to a meal before,
but I think I'm at the age
where I'm trying new things.

Slow things,
like being seen.

We got brunch.
She got a sausage and egg sandwich,
I got French toast.

*(I don't even like French toast,
it was just the only thing I understood
how to pronounce on the menu.)*

Still,
I ate the whole thing.
Even though it was kind of soggy
and weirdly sweet.

Big bites,
buying myself seconds
to build the next sentence.

My chest ached
when she let me try a bite of her food.
That's something I've only ever seen
couples do on TV.

She got up to use the bathroom.
Then again,
then again.

I told myself she probably
just had a small bladder,

or maybe she had coffee,
nerves,
or maybe she wanted to leave
but didn't know how to say it.

The check came
and she looked at me,
the waitress did too
and silently slid it my way.

And something ancient,
something shameful,
perhaps toxic,
still warm in me
felt *proud*.

Like we looked good,
like we looked real,
like I could pass
for the kind of man
who picks up the bill
without flinching.

My card didn't decline.
Thank God.
I had four dollars and thirty-six cents left
when I got home.

Even though my bones ached,
I felt a newfound gratitude
that I worked two jobs
so I could sit in that sunlit café
to buy someone this lovely
something as simple as brunch.

It had taken four hours to get dressed,
something that said

Man Enough for Myself

masculine,
but not too manly.

Not too girly,
but maybe
a little girly.
(If she liked that.)

Did she notice my missing tooth?
Did my hair look silly in the wind?
Should I have worn my glasses?

I wore black on black,
denim on top,
tried not to try too hard.
(I tried too hard.)

She said she liked my shirt,
I forgot to compliment hers
and maybe I forgot to compliment her at all.

Yet there she was
at the window table,
waiting for me.

How do you choose one thing
to compliment
when someone looks
as good as she does?

I was glad I wore my shoes
that gave me an extra inch.

My chest swelled
when her eyes looked up at me
and she commented
on how tall I was.

Donatello Dreakford

I think I'm realizing
I want someone as small as her
more than I thought.

That night I dreamed
of lifting someone up
on my shoulders at a concert,
of holding someone in my lap,
of tucking them beneath my arm
like they were made
for that space.

I don't know when I started
craving that kind of closeness,
but now I don't know
how to want
anything else.

When my friend asked how it went
I said,
"I think okay?"

We talked for three hours.
That's good, right?

She didn't bolt
during the awkward silences,
didn't fake a call,
didn't escape.

She stayed.

She told me she hasn't dated much either,
that she'd been single for years.

That made me feel better.
More even.

Man Enough for Myself

Like maybe we were both
just figuring it out as we went.

I asked all the questions
the internet told me to.

Even when it was time to part
I wanted more.
More to learn,
more time.

I followed her to the bus stop,
stayed 'til it came.
Asked her to get coffee after
because I couldn't say goodbye yet.

I hope it read
as endearing,
not desperate.

She's too beautiful,
too small,
to be left alone on that side of town.

And maybe
somewhere deep in me,
I knew.

That this could've been the last time.

Maybe the date didn't go
as well as I hoped,
and maybe the bus stop
was the last moment
I'd get to be close to her.

Still,
I'm happy I got to go.

Donatello Dreakford

To learn about her,
to learn what first dates feel like.

It's still unconfirmed
if I'll ever get a second,
but the way she responded to my
"I had a great time, hope you got home safe!"
message,

softly,
sweetly,
warmly,

is enough hope for now.

Enough space
to dream
about the next one.

Man Enough for Myself

(In case you were wondering, I never saw her again.)

Donatello Dreakford

The Man I Waited For

I used to think pleasure was a trick,
a way to keep me quiet.

That hands were proof of power,
and bodies were trophies
to be claimed.

I carried the weight of those nights
like a lock around my skin.
I thought desire was proof
of how easily I could be broken.

So I left myself untouched.
I left myself hollow.
I moved through my body
like a man in name only,
the word never matching the flesh.

It took years
before I was willing to stay,
before I could press my palm
to my own chest
and not flinch at the echo.

Years before I could look at myself undressed
and see a man worth touching.

Alone,
I began again.

Slow.

Palms across my stomach,
my thighs,
my chest.

Donatello Dreakford

Not rushing to erase anything,
just learning to arrive.

Breath after breath,
I found new ways to hold myself.

Every shiver was a small forgiveness,
every tremor a door unlocked.

The rhythm carried me forward
past shame,
past silence,
past the memory
of hands that hurt me.

What I felt building inside me
wasn't destruction,
but proof.

That I had survived,
that I had grown into a body
I could want.

That desire could belong to me
without guilt tying it down.

When I came,
it wasn't an ending.
It was a return.

Not disappearing,
not undone,
but full,
certain,
alive in my own skin.

Afterward,
the quiet wasn't heavy.
It didn't taste like loss.

Man Enough for Myself

It was mine.
It was release.

I touched myself into a man
who deserved to be here,
who could love without fear of breaking,
who had taken his body back
one breath,
one shiver,
one pulse at a time.

I became the first man
to touch me gently,
to press desire into my body
without taking anything from it.

The first man to love me
with patience,
with reverence,
with passion
that did not wound.

I became the man I had always needed.
The man who touched me first was me.

By the time someone else reached for me,
I wasn't waiting to be rescued.
I wasn't empty.
I was already whole.

I already knew my body
was mine to love first.

From there,
everything else could begin.

Donatello Dreakford

About Tina

By the time I met Tina, I didn't think love, real love, was something meant for me. I had already made peace with the idea that I was too complicated, too tired, too shaped by what I had done to survive. This book holds so much of that: the hunger, the harm, the years of being touched wrong, used up, left behind, and looked through. I spent a long time believing that love was just another thing to endure. That safety was a story other people got to live in.

Then came this person, with softness in their eyes and sharpness in their wit. With tenderness that wasn't performative or loud. Just present. Consistent. Startlingly real. They didn't flinch when I was quiet. They didn't try to save me. They just saw me: not because they wanted to fix me, but simply because they wanted to, because being with me was enough.

They gave me a different kind of love. One that didn't punish. One that didn't ask me to give more than I had. One that made it safe to want things. To rest. To be seen in my entirety: mess, grief, boyhood and all. The kind of care they give is quiet, steady, and real.

They taught me that love doesn't have to hurt to be true. That gentleness isn't weakness. That I can be cared for in ways that don't mimic control. That someone can learn my rhythms without trying to rewrite them.

Their love is quiet, but it's not small. It shows up in acts no one applauds. The kind that doesn't make it into movies, but saves lives anyway. They sew red hearts into my ripped clothes. They hand me a new toothbrush before I've even realized the old one is gone. They keep me steady without making me feel managed. For maybe the first time in my life, I don't feel like I have to earn every inch of tenderness I receive.

Tina has helped me unlearn the panic I used to call love. They're teaching me how to be still inside it. How to stay. They've changed the way I understand touch. The way I receive love, and the way I give it back. I've had to rewrite my entire idea of what a relationship can be. Not because they asked me to, but because being with them showed me it was possible.

It's not that I finally found someone who made me feel whole. It's that I finally feel whole enough to love someone from a place that isn't rooted in fear.

This section is for them.

These poems aren't just about Tina. They're about what their love revealed in me. What it helped me reclaim. What it allowed me to believe in again. This is the part of my story where I stop surviving and start choosing. Where I write about love not as a longing, but as a life I get to live. I didn't believe love like this was possible, especially not for someone like me. Yet here we are. I'm learning slowly but surely that I can let love in without disappearing inside it.

I. Last First Date

We met at my favorite theater.

The one with shaky seats
and screen burned walls,
where I always sit alone
in the same row,
in the same seat,
my church made from flickering light.

I had never let anyone into that sanctuary,
but there she was.

Just a little taller than I imagined,
stepping through the entrance
like she'd always belonged
in my quiet world.

When our eyes met,
my breath caught
like the hush in a theater
before the first note breaks the dark.

She looked at me
with warmth,
and I searched her face
for something wrong.

Some flicker of disinterest,
some subtle wince,
anything to prove
that I had read this all wrong.

But there was nothing,
only softness.

Donatello Dreakford

Only the terrifying miracle
of being wanted
exactly as I am.

We arrived late,
missed the first few minutes.
I lied and said
she hadn't missed much
just to keep her close,
to buy time
to explain everything
she'd ever want to know.

I was grateful for the darkness.
Grateful that the screen
lit her cheekbones
and not my trembling hands.

Even someone like me,
dense,
hesitant,
accustomed to missed signals
could feel her enthusiasm
in the way she leaned in.

The way her body
answered mine.

Her arm slowly curled around mine.
Her head found my shoulder.
I kept my face forward
like I wasn't unraveling
at every gentle touch.

It took me three quarters
of the movie
to take her hand.

Man Enough for Myself

Once I did,
I had to count my breaths
just to remember
how to stay alive.

Eight hundred and fifty-six.

That's how many more it took
for the credits to roll,
for her to let go,
and for the world to restart.

I didn't let go
until the usher asked us to leave.

And when I did,
the cold of her absence
hit me like a truth
I had no name for.

She asked to keep the night going.

I said yes,
of course, yes.

We walked arm-in-arm to her car
and my stomach churned
thinking of my messy room,
a space too real
for someone this incandescent.

(It wasn't clean.
She said it was fine,
I chose to believe her.)

We sat on my floor
cross-legged
playing my favorite icebreaker game

Donatello Dreakford

while the hours spun
like warm laundry.

Every question she answered
felt like a key,
a name,
a door,
and I collected them
like sacred artifacts.

If she was going to be
as pivotal to my life
as I already suspected,
then every detail mattered.

I listened
like I was studying scripture,
and I swear
she listened to me
with that same care.

As the night softened
and my nerves gave way
to something quieter,
she crawled into my lap
like a cat.

Graceful,
and certain that space
was made just for her.

Then it was.

Maybe it always had been.

She showed me pictures
of her three cats,
and I held her

Man Enough for Myself

like a thing
too precious to scare off.

When she relaxed into me,
melted her head
against my chest,
I almost cried.

My arms have felt empty
since the moment
she left them.

At almost three in the morning
she said she had to go,
but didn't want to.

Selfishly,
I wanted to keep her
right there forever.

Instead,
I made sure she was awake enough
to drive home safe.

(I let her stay
a few extra minutes,
just long enough
to study the puff of her cheeks
as she leaned into her arms.
To memorize
every flicker
of her resting face.)

I wrapped my jacket around her shoulders
and as I walked her to her car
she reapplied her lip gloss,
like the rest of the night:

Donatello Dreakford

not subtle,
not shy,
an invitation written in shimmer.

When we said goodbye
she looked at me
like she was handing me a chance.

This time,
finally,
I took it.

Our lips met.

A spark,
then a fire.

Not some shy brushing,
but a moment
that cracked something open.

As if my body
remembered
what it was made for.

Like all those movies
hadn't been lying after all.

It was brief
but it was real,
and I knew with a clarity
I've never had before
that I was going to fall in love.

Not maybe,
not someday,
now.

Man Enough for Myself

And strangely,
instead of fear
I felt light.

Even if she changes her mind.

Even if this isn't
the beginning
of forever.

Just *knowing*
this kind of love
exists,
that my heart is capable of it,
is enough
to make me hope.

Because I've been on
first dates before,
only three now.

Some lovely,
some painful,
most forgettable.

But this?

This is the first time
I've been *sure*
it won't be the last.

And I will do
whatever it takes
to make this
my last
first
date.

II. Asymmetrical

The first day we met
we ended up tangled on the floor of my room,
three weeks post-op.

I was still tender,
stitched up and reshaped,
my chest not yet mine,
not fully.

She pressed against me,
her body curling close
like none of that mattered,
like I was already enough.

I wasn't supposed to
let her lean on my chest,
wasn't supposed to
sleep on my side so soon,
wasn't supposed to
risk the soft places
still healing underneath,
but I did.

Because at that moment,
it felt worth it.

After a while
I noticed it.

A swelling under the skin,
warm,
puffy,
a little sore.

Man Enough for Myself

My body quietly collecting fluid,
making a space
I hadn't planned for.

At the clinic
they ran the ultrasound wand over my chest,
and there it was blinking back at me
from the screen,
a dark pocket,
small but certain
sitting beneath the surface.

A *seroma*.

I watched
as they slid the needle in,
felt the dull pressure
as they dug gently
for the right spot.

Ten ccs of fluid
drawn from my body,
lifted away
and still
it wasn't finished.

A week later
I was back,
but this time
there was no more fluid.

Just a hard knot of scar tissue
setting itself in place,
claiming the space
the seroma left behind.

Donatello Dreakford

And overtime
the swelling shrank,
but it never fully disappeared.

That side stayed
just a little different,
just uneven enough
to remind me
that something had happened there.

Now when I touch
that part of my body,
I think about
how love arrived
in the middle of all this.

Before I had the chance
to feel finished.

Before I knew
what this new skin
was supposed to be.

The seroma is fading,
softening,
disappearing,
day by day.

I can't help but wonder
if love will do the same.

Because the body
takes what it needs,
lets go of the rest,
heals whether we ask it to
or not.

Man Enough for Myself

But when my skin
forgets the swelling,
when the scar tissue
shrinks into memory,
I hope it still holds
the shape of that moment.

A mark
and a reminder
that even though I am permanently asymmetrical,
even though things didn't go exactly as planned,
I learned to love
what was left behind.

III. Little Birds

Little birds never told me
to keep my heart guarded.

They didn't have to.
I was born with the fences built in,
taught myself to flinch
before I even learned what love was.

I've always expected
the people I want
to want someone else.

Little birds never whispered
be careful,
or *don't hope too hard*,
that voice came from inside.

It sounded a lot like survival.

It sounded a lot like me
alone in my room,
trying to make peace
with being too much
and never enough
at the same time.

But then you showed up,
and suddenly
the birds weren't the only thing with wings.

You made softness feel safe,
you made staying feel possible.

I didn't expect you.
I didn't expect
the way you look at me

Man Enough for Myself

like I've always been good,
like I've always been worthy,
like I didn't have to earn it.

Now I find myself thinking about you
the way people talk about spring
when they've just made it through a long winter.

You don't have to worry
about scaring me,
I don't run from warmth anymore,
not when it's you.
Not when it feels this right.

I may not know how to say
I love you
without my voice shaking,
but I do know
that I'm not going anywhere.

You've quieted a part of me
I thought would never stop echoing,
and if little birds still circle overhead
they're just watching.

Wings tucked in
as I choose you again,
and again,
and again.

IV. The Way I Say It

I didn't want to rush it,
not because I don't feel it,
but because you're precious to me.

Your heart is something
I never want to mishandle,
and sure
maybe I've been protecting mine too,
but mostly
I've been thinking about yours.

About how people talk,
how people watch
how someone like me
might look like too much
to the ones who love you,
especially after what the last one put you through.

I don't ever want to be someone
you have to defend,
I want to be someone
you never have to explain.

I've thought I was in love before
but it always came
with shrinking,
with second-guessing,
with becoming a version of myself
that was easier for someone else to hold.

But you?
You don't ask me to be easier,
you just hold me.

Man Enough for Myself

I didn't realize how much I needed that
until I caught myself relaxing
in the small moments
I never used to notice.

You scrub my back in the shower
like it's the most natural thing in the world.

You lotion me after,
laugh when I flinch
like I'm not still stunned
by how gently you love.

You keep my toothbrush ready,
keep me in routine
without pressure,
you make the rest of life feel easier too.

When we're apart,
I don't know how I went so long
without this kind of care.

I love cooking for you.
I love driving you places
even when I complain about the traffic.
I love when you pack my lunches,
and sew little red hearts
into my clothes when they rip.

Your care shows up
in all the places people call small,
but nothing is small with you.

And yes,
I know
I haven't said the words yet.

Not out loud.

Donatello Dreakford

But I do love you.
Of course I do.
How could I not?

You make it feel easy to.

I feel it in the mornings
when your face is soft and puffy from sleep,
and you look so peaceful
I could cry just from being near you.

I feel it when my clothes smell like your house,
and I'm reminded I have somewhere
to come back to.

I feel it in every one of your freckles,
I count them in my head
like I'm trying to memorize the sky.

You've heard the words
even if I haven't spoken them.

You hear it
in the way I stay,
in the way I listen,
in how I reach for you without thinking,
in how I remember the things you say
even when you think I'm not paying attention.

I always am,
because it's you.

There's nothing temporary about this,
no act,
no performance.

Just me,
here,
trying to learn how to be loved like this,

Man Enough for Myself

and doing everything I can
to give it back
the way you deserve.

And when I do finally say it,
really say it,
you won't be surprised.

You'll just smile
like you've known the whole time.

Because I've been saying it
in the way I hold you,
in the way I come home to you,
in the way I've been writing it
across every ordinary day
we've made sacred
just by doing them together.

V:
What Remains

This is what I carried out of it all,
what's left is still me.

About D'Mon

D'Mon was my drag persona. She came to life in 2021, when I started walking the runway category in ballroom. I was earlier in my medical transition then. There wasn't a subcategory I fit into cleanly, I didn't pass as a butch queen, definitely couldn't blend in with cisgender women, and I wasn't a femme queen either: So I carved my own lane. I hid among the drag queens, because it felt safer to be someone else.

She became a version of me I didn't know I needed. A little tragic, a little dangerous. Beautiful in a way that was uncomfortable to witness, like a car crash you couldn't look away from. I like to say she was what I might've become if I had never transitioned.

Somehow, she made it work. I won Overall Runway of the year two years in a row in my local Kiki Scene here in Seattle. Later, I started performing in nightclubs. I figured it would come naturally. I used to be a stripper. I thought, *this'll be easy*. It wasn't. I was terrible when I started. But I got better, not because I was especially gifted, but because I was stubborn enough to stay.

Ballroom was the first place I ever saw a room full of black trans men and women. A whole lineage of us. Laughing, strutting, thriving. It shifted something in me. I saw who I could become. I was affirmed, lifted up, poured into by other black trans people who understood the shape of my becoming. Even if I don't walk anymore, I still carry those people who are now my queer family, and those moments with me. They gave me something solid to reach for, and they loved me in ways that made returning to myself possible.

I'm far from a fixture in the Seattle drag scene, or ballroom. I'm not well known. I'm already fading out, and that's okay. I just hope a few queers out there remember me. Lip syncing to sad music. Holding myself under the basement lights at Kremwerk. I'm sure the few reading this book know me through her.

Donatello Dreakford

This poem is for her. A farewell. A tribute. A quiet thank you for what she gave me, what I made it through wearing her name, and the pain she made beautiful just long enough to bear.

D'Mon

Sometimes,
I miss performing.

Not the bars,
not the green rooms,
not the way my name got
mispronounced,
forgotten,
chewed up by mouths
that smiled too big
and saw too little.

I don't miss how the wrong people
got too close.

How hands landed like claims,
how silence was mistaken for grace,
how I learned to laugh
through violation.

I don't miss wondering
if I was loved
or just useful.

If I was booked
because I mattered,
or because I filled a quota
on a lineup
and made the show look diverse.

But I do miss the moment
before the music starts.

Donatello Dreakford

That hush,
the lights dimming,
that breath
right before I became someone else.

I miss choosing who I'd be
for three to six minutes.

Dramatic,
divine,
a disaster
wrapped in rhinestones
and hurt.

I miss the trance of it all.

The train rides home,
headphones in,
looping the same chorus
until I could see it.

Me,
commanding a room,
crying through a smile
in a costume sewn
from every heartbreak I swallowed
just to get through the week.

I miss the release,
making people feel something
because I couldn't stand
to feel it alone.

A room full of strangers
forced to sit with my sadness,
and clap for it.

Man Enough for Myself

Because in real life
no one lets me fall apart
so loudly.

So,
I stopped.

I stepped out of the spotlight
to stop bleeding
for people who never brought bandages.

I chose quiet,
I chose what was left of me.

For a while,
I felt like I was letting everyone down.
Like I'd failed,
walked away too soon,
and owed the audience
one more show.

I then realized
I didn't give up,
I just stopped needing applause
to know that whatever I do matters.

Maybe that's the mark of a real artist.

Not the performance,
but the decision to create
from a place of truth,
not hunger.

The truth is,
I started performing
to cover myself up.

I started crossdressing
to hide how much I hated my own reflection.

Donatello Dreakford

I wore femininity
like camouflage,
like a distraction.

It made people cheer,
made them look,
though they were never really looking at me.

Somewhere along the way
I realized I was disappearing
under the lashes,
under the wigs,
under the paint,
I was vanishing
even as the crowd screamed my name.

It's not that performing isn't for me.

It's just that now,
I finally feel whole
as myself.

Just Donatello.

No act.
No alter ego.
No need to twist my truth
into something easier to swallow.

Maybe that's why I started writing.

Now I dress my feelings in ink
instead of lashes.

I stage performances on paper,
whisper monologues into zines,
and hope they echo
in someone's chest
on a quiet afternoon.

Man Enough for Myself

(Maybe yours.)

Because I still want to be looked at.

Not stared at,
not consumed,
but *seen.*

Maybe that's what I've been trying to do all along,
get people to look past the spectacle
into the soft aching thing underneath.

To those who watched me become something,
who waited through the silence,
who missed me without saying it,
thank you.

You were always the reason it felt worth it.

And if you've wondered where I went,
if you've waited for a return,
this is it.

This page is my stage now,
this pen my mic,
and I'm still performing.

Still shining,
still trying to make *something*
out of my story.

Only this time
I'm doing it without hiding,
without asking,
without apology.

Because now
I'm man enough for myself,
and I still want to be seen.

Donatello Dreakford

Donatello Dreakford

Still Here

It's taken time
to loosen the grip
of a hope I mistook
for something owed.

To admit that love,
or at least the kind I wanted,
was never mine to begin with.

You didn't choose me.

Not because I wasn't kind,
or close,
or there,
but because when you look at me
you still see someone I've shed.

You don't mean to,
it's not cruel,
it's just memory
doing what it does best.

Clinging to an outline
I've long since outgrown.

Holding onto a softness
I no longer wear.

I've become something new,
a man in full,
and I am proud of that.

But sometimes I wonder
if I lost your warmth
the moment I stopped fitting
the shape you once found comfort in.

Man Enough for Myself

I used to hope
you'd see me again
in this new light.

Stopped twisting myself
into maybe.

Others will love me
without a history in their eyes,
without a past
clouding the present.

And still,
I miss the way
you held me once
without hesitation.

I miss the version of us
where your hand found mine
without thinking,
just instinct,
where I was just someone
you trusted to be real.

I don't chase anymore,
but if someday
your eyes soften around who I've become,
if you ever reach out
not to remember,
but to *know* me
as I am now,
I'll still be here.

Rent

Why is everything
so fucking expensive?

I work all the time
and still
I'm running out of breath
before the month runs out of bills.

I don't go out,
don't splurge,
don't buy clothes,
eat out,
or do anything *but* survive.

And yet,
the numbers keep sinking
like I'm bleeding out slow.

How am I supposed to pay rent this month?

How am I supposed to see without contacts,
eat without fixing my teeth,
function without the meds
that keep me from unraveling entirely?

Why does it cost so much
just to be alive?

Why do I have to buy
my right to breathe,
to sleep inside,
to stay sane
in a world that would rather I disappear?

How is it that shelter,
something even stray animals find,

Man Enough for Myself

comes with a price tag
I've never been able to afford?

I walk past tents on sidewalks
and my body *remembers*.

Remembers what it's like
to be that close to gone,
to be the thing people step around,
the background noise of a city that only sees
what it can use or throw away.

Once the world learns to look through you
it forgets you were ever there.

But this didn't start with bills.

This started when I was a kid
asking my mother what was for dinner
and getting *"I don't know"*
or worse,
rage.

We didn't have a washing machine
or a car to get to the laundromat.

I went to school in the same dirty clothes
week after week,
shamed by my peers
and taught that poverty was contagious.

We had no heat,
no hot water.
I took cold showers every day
and told myself
that was normal.

Donatello Dreakford

Sometimes we didn't have electricity
so the food in the fridge spoiled,
then rotted.

Then came the maggots,
larvae squirming through
what used to be nourishment,
until we just stopped opening the door.

Our fridge became a coffin,
the kitchen a graveyard.

Dinner was a can of corn
or my favorite,
sliced pears in syrup.

Cold,
metallic,
eaten straight out of the can
because there was nothing else.

But every so often
my mother would come home with fast food,
bags of hot fries and pizza boxes
bought with the child support money
my dad sent to feed us,
and wouldn't share.

She'd eat alone
behind a locked door,
while we starved in the next room.

I'd sit there,
my stomach hollow and screaming,
feeling the kind of betrayal
that etches itself into your bones.

Man Enough for Myself

That money was meant to save us,
instead she spent it
on Newports,
on bottles,
on drugs.

I grew up jealous of her vices
because they got more of her love
than I ever did.

My room hadn't grown with me,
it was a rat feces filled tomb
frozen in time.

Just a mattress
sunken on the floor,
no bedframe,
no comfort,
just me and the walls
that never changed.

After a while we had no car,
when I missed the bus
I walked to school
one hour each way,
alone.

I started working at 14,
forged my birth certificate
so I could get a job.

Survival doesn't care if you're old enough.

The summer CPS came
was one of the hottest I remember.

Donatello Dreakford

No air conditioning,
just heavy air and heat
that stuck to the walls like sweat.

I looked at the thermostat,
92 degrees inside.
We were all melting.

The house smelled like rot,
like heat,
and mold,
and bodies,
and decay.

So when the police knocked,
and CPS stood behind them,
and they finally took us away,
I didn't cry.

Because even then
I knew what we were living in
wasn't living.

I've been homeless on and off since adolescence.

Slept on couches,
slept in my car,
slept outside,
sold my body when I had nothing else left.

I let men take what they wanted,
because rent was due.

Because hunger doesn't wait.

Because pain feels better
than starving.

And now?

Man Enough for Myself

Now I have two jobs,
work over 50 hours a week
and still barely scrape by.

I can't sell my body anymore.

I'm too worn,
too wrong,
too masculine to pull the johns I used to,
too trans to fit anyone's fantasy,
too human to be commodified,
too tired to even try.

And I'm ashamed.

Ashamed,
but grateful.

Grateful for the food bank lines,
for community meals,
for friends passing back and forth the same twenty dollars
when I don't even have the strength to ask.

Because without them,
I'd be back outside.

And even now,
even with help,
I still feel like I'm failing.

Everyone else seems to be making it.

What am I missing?

Where are they getting their money?

What job do they have
that pays *more* than survival?

What door won't open for me?

Donatello Dreakford

I'm not lazy,
I'm not careless,
I'm just carrying the weight
of a whole life spent catching up.

Can someone teach me?

Can I join?

Can I just
have a little?

Not everything,
just enough
to rest.

To stop disappearing
while I'm still alive.

First Check After Zero

Then the next morning comes
and I am exactly $0 rich
and 98 hours tired.

This check isn't a reward,
it's proof I've survived again,
barely.

It's me saying
I want to live,
even if I'm not sure how.

I've got $8,165 in loans.
A corpse I signed for
just to escape.
Not for books,
but for distance.
Not for dorms,
but for silence.

Now it follows me,
dead weight
I drag from job to job,
city to city,
still wearing my old name
like a tag on its toe.

$1,046 in collections.
A credit card I maxed out
to fix a car I don't even have anymore.
I didn't plan to be alive long enough
to pay it back.
I bought time with borrowed money
and lost both.

Donatello Dreakford

Now it rots on my record
like something I left behind
that found its own way back.

$1,400 in taxes
from a year I barely made rent.
A year I was homeless
for more months than not.
I don't know how I owe them
when what I earned
was barely enough to survive.

Still, they found a way
to put a price on breath,
so now it grows like mold
on the ceiling of my future.

Rent is $755
and my storage unit is $89.
A mausoleum for a self I've outlived,
full of drag I don't wear
from numbers I'll probably never perform again.
Hangers, wigs, old duct-taped heels,
and costumes I built
when I still believed
being seen could save me.

Now I keep them locked away
like a version of myself
I can't decide to mourn or resurrect.

Utilities are $150.
To keep the lights on
and the memories out.

Man Enough for Myself

Sometimes I sit in the dark anyway.
Sometimes I leave every light burning
just to prove I'm still here.

Groceries, $125.
Most of it spoils.
I stack food in the fridge
like bodies in a potter's field,
unclaimed,
unwanted,
proof that I once tried
to prepare for a hunger
I couldn't name.

It comforts me,
this soft decay.

It reminds me of the house I ran from,
of rot that stayed quiet
when people didn't.

And still,
$1,132 lands in my account
every other Friday,
and every time
I split it open like a chest cavity,
sort the organs,
try to keep something alive.

Because I want a future
more than I want relief.

Because I've made it this far
and it's too late to turn back.

Because even if I never outrun the corpse
I am not laying down beside it.

Donatello Dreakford

Not yet.

Before the Knife

This won't fix everything.

It won't make you
perfect in the mirror
or erase every doubt.

Transformation is slow,
a long discipline of care.

But this is a step,
an important one,
yours.

You've waited years.

Wanting,
doubting,
explaining yourself
to people who never really got it.

This isn't just medical.
It's personal.
It's reclamation.

Still,
Flat don't mean free.

You'll still flinch,
still relearn to be touched,
how to want,
how to be wanted.

Yet this brings you closer
to comfort,
to clarity,
to a softness that doesn't feel like surrender.

Donatello Dreakford

Big moments can be quiet.
Life changing days
can feel ordinary.
Let that be enough.

Forget the pre-surgery goals.

The weight,
the muscle,
the imagined body
you thought you'd need to deserve this.

You're still showing up,
that is enough.

You've never been trapped in your body,
only in the way others chose to see it.
Now you get to define yourself.

Picture this:
a loose shirt clinging in the breeze,
ocean water on your bare chest,
a hug,
chest to chest,
nothing in the way.

These moments are real.
They are waiting.

Afterward

You braced for agony,
for breakdowns,
for grief.

Instead,
stillness.

Soft mornings,
a body doing
what it was always capable of,
peace showing up quietly.

For once the mirror
matches what you know.

All that fear,
all those years,
none of it mattered.

Twelve pounds
gone in a single day,
not one of them
worth contemplating.

You've gained it back
in good food,
slow evenings,
being fed by love
instead of hunger.

There is no real pain,
just a spark under your arm
where nerves whisper back to life.

Donatello Dreakford

Healing is stubborn,
subtle,
alive.

Your body is
resilient,
responsive,
kind.

Maybe it was never the enemy,
only misunderstood.

Two weeks in,
drains gone,
swelling down.

You pressed the fluid out yourself,
woke up the next morning
and saw your chest again.

Not perfect,
but real.

Yours.

The shame is fading,
so are the bruises.

Nothing dramatic,
just the ordinary miracle
of healing.

They let you keep your old breasts,
now pickled in a jar on the bookshelf.

If the book doesn't sell,
maybe you'll auction one off.

Even that weightlessness
feels like freedom.

Man Enough for Myself

Letting someone care for you
without needing to earn it
cracked something open.

That mattered more than you expected.

Ease is allowed.
Joy is allowed.
You don't have to earn peace through pain.

Maybe this isn't a new you.

Maybe it's the same one
who carried hunger,
who carried silence,
who carried hurt,
and survived anyway.

The one who learned
to live through grief,
to surface again.

Maybe this is just the you
who has always been here.

Known,
and finally free.

Donatello Dreakford

No Prize

As a kid I kept a picture of later.

Not fame,
only the hush that falls when the ones who hurt me
finally look up and wish they had been kind.

I told myself it would come if I held on hard enough,
that what cut me would turn into something bright.

Getting older, the truth comes clean without softness:
nothing I lived made me rare.

There is no prize for hurt,
no secret door.

Pain doesn't turn you into more,
it happens,
then it sits in your history like any other fact.

I learned that first in the ditch by highway 55.

One shoe turned toward the road,
a metallic taste in my mouth,
cars sounding far and not for me:

"The world can be beautiful
and not give a damn about you.
The sky can be loud,
and nobody comes."

I listened to my own breath
because there was nothing else to hear,
then I stood up and kept going.

Donatello Dreakford

I learn it again now with the manuscript open,
lamp on,
pages softened from being handled.

The same sentence returns
and it doesn't break anything.

It just sits beside me
while I cut a word,
move a line,
write my name once and leave it be.

I used to think everything I'd endured would add up to proof
that one day I'd become the answer.

But here we are:
me writing,
you reading,
two people with histories that don't crown us,
just people,
still here.

Maybe you know that picture too,
the one that promised the turn.

It kept us breathing when it had to.

And still,
the truth lands where it lands:
what happened is not a ticket,
not a sign,
not the reason we matter.

And then the weight lifts

Choosing ordinary
is how we stop letting harm write the headline.

Man Enough for Myself

We move it to the back of the book
and keep the day.

If we are not required to be extraordinary,
we can set the weight down.

If the world can be beautiful
and not give a damn about us,
then what happened isn't the center.

We step into a day that owes us nothing
and it is generous.

We are not rare; that is the point.
This is the freedom we almost didn't see.

Ordinary,
and ours.

About The Author

Donatello Dreakford is a Black trans artist, writer, and aspiring mortician. He has spent years making art in many forms, from the page to live performance, carrying with him the lessons and beauty of the drag and ballroom scenes.

His work is rooted in honesty and connection, shaped by experiences of poverty, queerness, chosen family, and the quiet persistence of staying. When he is not writing, he finds joy spending time with his partner and their three cats, mentoring younger artists, and holding close the people he loves. *Man Enough for Myself* is his first book.

www.ingramcontent.com/pod-product-compliance
Lightning Source LLC
Chambersburg PA
CBHW051622120626
46551CB00014B/1905